Getting A Handel On

Messiah

David W. Barber

SOUND AND VISION

TORONTO

Contents

Author's Note and Acknowledgements

It's with a certain amount of trepidation that one takes on so enormously popular and important a work as Handel's *Messiah*. But it's precisely because of its popularity that I'm sure *Messiah* will survive this irreverent yet affectionate little book of mine.

In keeping with the spirit of my previous books, the usual reminder applies. All the facts are accurate, the information here is true — or at least as true as I've been able to ascertain from all the various history and music books I've consulted. Since I wasn't actually there, I can only assume that others before me got their facts straight in the first place.

Once again, I'd like to thank the usual gang: Dave Donald for his witty cartoons, publisher Geoff Savage and Jacky Savage at Sound And Vision for all their efforts, and especially my wife, Judy Scott, for being a patient and valuable sounding board.

DWB
Westport, July 1994

Preface

I am an unabashed *Messiah* enthusiast and Handel fan. The prospect of performing *Messiah* always fills me with excitement, as each performance is a voyage of discovery. It's rather like walking in a favourite place where each day you can see things in a new light or notice new details. I normally direct the work from the harpsichord, just as Handel did. It is easy to feel Handel's spirit as I touch the keys and give life to page-bound notes.

I've often asked myself what it is that gives *Messiah* its enduring popular appeal. Perhaps a clue can be found in the *Dublin News-Letter*, 10 April 1742.

"Yesterday morning at the Musick Hall...there was a public Rehearsal of the Messiah...which in the opinion of the best Judges, far surpasses anything of the Nature, which has been performed in this or in any other Kingdom."

Ten years later one enthusiast wrote to a friend "As much as I detest fatigue and inconvenience I would ride forty miles in the wind and rain to be present at a performance of *Messiah* in London under the conduct of Handel."

Haydn, upon hearing the work for the first time, was moved to tears and exclaimed "He was the master of us all."

For me the appeal of the work lies in the directness with which we are made aware of Handel's humanity. In a good performance the music unites audience and musicians in a whole range of emotions. Gleefully Handel invites us to go astray in *All we like sheep*, before revealing the cost of such action in the last bars. How deeply he moves us in the heartrending aria *He was despised*. And how uplifted we feel by the *Hallelujah* chorus. Handel was well aware of the power of his *Messiah*.

When Lord Kinnoull complimented Handel on the "entertainment," Handel replied "I should be sorry if I only entertained them, I wish to make them better."

Handel knows his audience will arrive thinking of a hundred and one things, and his task is to get us to listen to the story. The overture settles us into our seats. Then Handel introduces an inspired touch. The tenor stands and sings, his first phrase containing only two words, "Comfort Ye." We settle back and start to listen.

I love this opening. It reminds me of "Listen with Mother," a BBC radio programme which I listened to as a child with my mother. Having announced the title of the story the storyteller always asked "Are you sitting comfortably? Then I'll begin."

Luckily *Messiah* is quite resilient. It needs to be, for such a frequently performed work is prey to all sorts of dangers. I've heard absolutely riveting performances of *Messiah*. But some performances I have found sanctimonious (too slow and solemn) over-fashionable (too fast and secular) or complacent (boring). There are many different versions, even rock and soul arrangements, parts of which I have enjoyed. In the end all that matters is that the power of the work shines through. That is a good performance.

Those who have laughed their way through David Barber's earlier books will know that there are a lot of facts lurking behind his irreverent humour. So if you want to get a "Handel" on *Messiah*, read on.

Meanwhile, after having written these words I can hardly wait to get back to Handel's music. At each performance of *Messiah* I feel with Haydn that "He was the master of us all."

Trevor Pinnock
London, August 1994

Dedication

For Judy (again), for everything we've been through.

CHAPTER 1

OVERTURE

Everybody's favourite oratorio

OVERTURE

HANDEL'S *MESSIAH* IS PROBABLY one of the best-loved, and certainly one of the best-known, works in the standard repertoire of "classical" music. [1]

Messiah had its first production in 1742, and it has now been performed almost every year since for more than two-and-a-half centuries. Like some hardy perennial, or maybe just a persistent weed, *Messiah* just keeps coming back, year after year.

Although Handel himself revived it frequently in the years leading up to his death, there was no performance of *Messiah* in 1744 and none again in '46 to '48. But these were just glitches. Since 1749, when it really got rolling, there probably hasn't been a year gone by when someone, *somewhere* didn't perform *Messiah*. [2]

---

[1] For a more detailed discussion of problems surrounding use of the term "classical," please see the chapter entitled "A Classic Problem" in my earlier book *If It Ain't Baroque: More Music History As It Ought To Be Taught*. I just haven't the energy to go over all of it again here, and besides, you'd be doing your bit to support a struggling author.

[2] If there has, I'd love to hear about it.

1

Music historian Stanley Sadie may be going a bit over-board when he calls *Messiah* "the greatest single work in the English language" (evidently married works need not apply), but there's no denying its many beautiful, inspiring or other-wise admirable moments. (There are also a few tiresome choruses I'd just as soon be without — *Their sound is gone out*, for instance, or *But thanks be to God* — but I realize I'm in the minority on this.)

Whatever its musical merits — and let's just say there's some room for argument here — there can be no denying that *Messiah* has an enormous popular appeal. Audiences and performers alike may love it because it's full of rousing choruses, flashy solo arias and some quieter moments that can, at least at the best of times, be genuinely poignant. Choir managers love it because you can almost be guaran-teed to draw a big crowd, and tickets are easier to sell than for the choir's next performance — that all-Schönberg pro-gram, say, or the concert version of Berg's *Wozzeck*.

Many musicians, both singers and instrumentalists, have what may be described as a love/hate relationship with *Mes-siah*. On the one hand, after performing it year in and year out they may be growing bored with having to do it again. But on the other hand it tends to be an easy gig, since after doing it a few times, you get to know the notes. (And if you haven't figured out the notes after the first four or five times, you're probably never going to get them.) [3]

All of this enormous popularity, not to mention its staying power, is a bit surprising for what was essentially a

[3] Trumpet players have it pretty easy. They get paid for a whole night's gig, but they only play in the *Hallelujah* chorus and a few others. Nice work if you can get it.

pot-boiler of a work the composer dashed off in about three weeks to fill time on some upcoming program, and in the hopes that it might bring him in some much-needed money. (By this time in his career, although a successful and respected composer, Handel was a bit strapped for cash.)

To be fair, it wasn't just the financial prospects that moved Handel. He could be as pragmatic and businesslike as the next fellow (in fact considerably more so than most), but he did have his more spiritual side. Although not much of a churchgoer in his youth and middle age, Handel in his later years could have won an award for faithful attendance. By then he was going twice a day, regular as clockwork, to the little church of St. George's, Hanover Square, around the corner from his house on Brook Street. There's nothing like impending death to inspire a little religious fervor.

As for the work itself, Handel once later remarked that, while composing the *Hallelujah* chorus, he felt "as if I saw God on his throne, and all his angels around him."

Or maybe it was just something he ate.

CHAPTER 2

ARTICLE OF FAITH

Correcting a misconception

ARTICLE OF FAITH

ONE OF THE REALLY BURNING questions about Handel's beloved masterpiece is what to call it.

Well, OK, maybe not a *really* burning question, along the lines of "Is there a God?" or "What is the meaning of life?" or even "Why does lousy weather always come on the weekends?" But it's enough of a question that not everybody knows the answer right away.

Go on, see for yourself. Ask the next 10 people you meet which is correct, to refer to it as *Messiah* or *The Messiah*. I'm willing to bet the answer won't be unanimous either way. It will make a great conversation-opener at your next party. (Well, maybe it depends on the kind of parties you go to.)

A lot of people go with *The Messiah*, feeling somehow that calling it just *Messiah* seems incomplete. They like having that definite article in front there — makes it seem more like the title of something, rather than just someone's name. Maybe they think the definite article gives the work more authority: not just any old garden-variety, run-of-the-mill messiah, but *THE* Messiah.

Maybe they think that otherwise we might confuse it with a *Messiah* by some other composer, less important than the great Handel. (That's one nifty way around the dilemma, by the way. You can just refer to it all the time as "Handel's *Messiah*," although this does somehow imply that there are others out there we don't mean to be talking about.) [1]

In fact, this little issue has become something of a litmus test among musicians and music lovers. In general, your average person on the street may be quite happy to use the "the." But musicians themselves, those with serious musical training or just those who want to pretend they have, usually call it simply *Messiah*.

Musicians — and especially would-be musicians — tend, let's face it, to be a pretty snobby bunch. Nothing makes them feel more superior than making you feel they know something that you don't. And what better way than to argue obscure points of musical history, especially if they can bring in foreign grammar and a little philology to back up their arguments?

Myself, I'm a *Messiah* man, for a number of reasons (not the least may be a little snobbery). First of all — and here's the bit about grammar and philology — *Messiah* is a Hebrew term of respect meaning "the anointed," or "the chosen one." So calling anyone "the Messiah" would be redundant, since the definite article is already built in to the title: "the the chosen one" just doesn't make sense. [2]

---

[1] To the best of my knowledge, no other composers have decided to run the risk, sensibly avoiding calling any of their own works *Messiah*. Who needs the headache?

[2] Isn't there a pop group called The The? That's not to be confused with Mister Mister or Duran Duran.

But more to the point, Handel himself never used the "the." [3] On the title page and whenever he wrote about his work in letters or elsewhere, he called it simply *Messiah*.

So I figure, if that's what he wants to call it, that's what we should call it, too. After all, he's older than we are, and he deserves a little respect.

---

[3] Well, OK, there was that one time in his will. But he was old and on his death bed, for pity's sake. Give the guy a break.

CHAPTER 3

COMING TO GRIPS
WITH HANDEL

Handel's father dreamed of a career in law for little George

Coming to Grips with Handel

CONSIDERING THAT HE WENT on to write "the greatest single work in the English language," Handel's life began simply enough — almost hardly worth mentioning, really. He liked to wait for the right moment before making a big splash.

Handel was born into a simple middle-class family in February 1685 — on the 23rd, in case you were planning to send a card — and baptised the following day. The church registry gives his name as Georg Friederich Händel. Later in life, after he'd moved to England and become a British subject, he changed it to George Frideric Handel. (Yes, it would be easier all around if he'd gone all the way and Anglicized his given names to George Frederick — but he didn't, so there you have you it. Spelling was never his strong suit, anyway.)

Händel, or Handel, was born in Halle, a small German town on a lovely river bank, not far from Leipzig. The town's full name is *Halle an der Saale*, but the only people who call it that are picky Germans and tourism promoters.

Speaking of being picky, I should point out that at that time Halle wasn't really a part of Germany. It was in Saxony, which in those days was sort of a separate little duchy. Saxony started out as a region, became a kingdom, then a duchy, then was annexed by Prussia for a while. (The Prussians were fond of annexing their neighbors. It gave them an occasion to wear those funny spiked helmets they liked so much.) Much later, between the First and Second World Wars, Saxony joined in as part of the flourishing Weimar Republic, but that didn't last for long.

After the Second World War that area of Saxony became part of East Germany. But now that the Berlin Wall is gone, it's just part of one big Germany again. Funny how that works out.

Anyway, through most of the 17th century the people who worry about this sort of thing would have considered Halle part of Saxony, which had its own bigwig, called an "Elector," who held court there, complete with theatres, music, dancing and general merriment. Halle in those days was a fun place to be. (Strangely enough, despite the title, being Elector was not an elected position. It was something you inherited from your parents, along with the horses and the family silverware.)

Actually, Saxony was only controlled by the Elector of Saxony until just before Handel was born. In 1680, after the Peace of Westphalia, Halle was handed over to the Elector of Brandenburg next door, and he didn't quite know what to do with it. But even though they had a new Elector, the people of Halle weren't about to call themselves Brandenburgians, or Brandenburgers, or whatever. They still considered themselves Saxons, no matter what some silly old treaty tried to say. They were stubborn that way.

An enormous amount of land changed hands thanks to the Peace of Westphalia. (And don't ask where Westphalia is. We've haven't got time for that right now.) Under the terms of the Treaty of Münster and the Treaty of Osnabrück, Sweden got the Baltic coast, France got Alsace and most of Lorraine, and the German princes agreed to stop trying to kill each other — which seemed the most anybody could hope for from them. Nobody was entirely happy, but at least it brought an end to the Thirty Years' War. And about time, too. [1]

Halle was an industrial town, chiefly known for the mining of salt, potash and lignite, a form of brown coal more important in those days than it is now. When Handel said it was time to go back to the salt mines, he knew what he was talking about.

Having sort of inherited it, the new Elector of Brandenburg, Duke Johann Adolf of Saxe-Weissenfels, didn't really like Halle and had no intention of living there. So he up and moved his whole court to Weissenfels, where he figured he'd have a better time. From then on, as one historian rather quaintly puts it, "Halle relapsed from courtly splendour into the dull monotony of burgherdom." Well, that's the way it goes.

Anyway, for our purposes, it would save us all a lot of trouble if we just agreed to say that Handel was born in

---

[1] The Thirty Years' War ran from 1618 to 1648, so it actually did last for 30 years. The Hundred Years' War, on the other hand, ran from 1337 to 1457, or 120 years. Maybe they were too busy fighting to count properly.

Germany and leave it at that. OK? (J.S. Bach was born in Thuringia, which is a whole different story. Don't get me started on that.) [2]

Handel's family had come to Halle from Breslau in the early 1600s. His grandfather, Valentin Handel, was a coppersmith who got himself elected to the town council and went on to become the town's official bread weigher. [3]

Tracing Handel's lineage can be tricky at times, since, as music historian Herbert Weinstock points out, members of the Handel family "were remarkable for the inconsistency with which they spelled their name." It could be Händel, Hendel, Hendtler, Händler, Hendel, Handl, Hendall and a few more besides. Evidently no one in the family was much at spelling.

Handel's father, old Georg Handel, was Halle's own Horatio Alger story, having started out as the Elector's valet. By the time Handel was born, he'd worked his way up to the post of official court barber-surgeon. (Georg was 62 when the young Handel was born, so he wasn't exactly a spring chicken. He'd had a while to get there.)

Nobody much thinks of becoming a barber-surgeon nowadays, but at that time it was a perfectly respectable occupation. (Though potentially dangerous. You wanted to make sure when you sat down in the chair just exactly what sort of cutting old Georg was expecting to do.) [4]

---

[2] Keeping abreast of German political geography took real talent in the 17th century. Nowadays it's something of a lost art.

[3] Germans in the 17th century took their bread weighing very seriously — almost as seriously as they took their political geography.

[4] Monteverdi's father had been a barber-surgeon, too. I'm not exactly sure what this proves, but it must prove something.

The Handel family lived in Giebechenstein, a Halle suburb, in a little house known as *zum gelben Hirsch*, or The Yellow Stag, which had once been a tavern. Georg Handel, no fool, had lobbied hard to keep the liquor licence, and made a tidy profit on the side selling wine to soldiers and other passersby. Maybe the fact that he grew up in a tavern explains Handel's later extreme fondness for eating and drinking. An infamous caricature by the artist Goupy shows the great composer, with a pig's snout, sitting down at an organ overloaded with food. When Handel saw it he was not amused.

That would be Joseph Goupy, a French-born English artist who specialized in etchings, miniatures and fan-painting. Fan-painting was big in the 18th century, but nowadays you could hardly make a living at it. He was the nephew of Lewis Goupy, another fan-painter, whose biography states that he "painted portraits in oil, and also drew in crayons." (I drew in crayons, too, when I was a child. But you don't see me bragging about it to *The Dictionary of National Biography*.) Joseph Goupy's caricature seems especially ungrateful when you consider that he made about £100 off Handel by selling him his South Sea shares. [5]

If you were to go to that Halle street today looking for The Yellow Stag, you'd find a simple house all decorated with fancy carving, a bust of the composer with the names of his famous oratorios — including *Messiah* — and a plaque that proclaims it as "Handel's Birthplace."

---

[5] "South Sea shares" might make the basis for a nifty tongue-twister. How about this: "Should South Sea shares sell short, surely she'd seem slightly shaded."

He was born in the house next door. (What can I say? Some-body goofed.)

Old Georg Handel was a well-meaning father but rather stern, and he had no particular interest in music — certainly not enough to let his son study it. The boy was going to become a lawyer, and that was that. (Other composers also had fathers who wanted them to become lawyers, including Schütz, Schumann and Tchaikovsky, each of whom studied law for a while. Elgar worked briefly as a clerk in a law office. Dvorak's father just wanted him to become a butcher.)

Fortunately for our hero, Handel's mother, Dorothea, was a bit more sympathetic. To hear Handel tell it, she helped the young boy smuggle a clavichord into the attic, where he would practise late at night after everyone else had gone to sleep. (The clavichord is a portable keyboard instrument that resembles a small piano or harpsichord. It's so quiet you can hardly hear it from a few feet away, much less way up in the attic through all the snoring.) This sounds almost too good to be true, if you ask me. But that was Handel's story and he stuck to it, so what can we say? [6]

Handel might have remained just a closet clavichordist but for a lucky break when he was about seven (some say nine) years old. He'd gone with his father to the palace of the duke ("Short back and sides, Georg, same as before") and wandered into the chapel, where he began playing the organ. The duke, who had the good sense to be impressed rather than angry, made the boy's father promise to let him have further music lessons.

---

[6] In some versions of the story, it was Handel's Aunt Anna who ran the clavichord-smuggling operation. Take your pick. It's all the same to me.

So Handel began taking music lessons from Friedrich Wilhelm Zachau (or Zachow), a local church organist and composer. Neither John Mainwaring, Handel's first biographer, nor Friedrich Chrysander, the editor of Handel's collected works, thinks much of Zachau as a musician (his music was "innocuous and trifling," they said, and "never rose to great heights"). But evidently he was better than that — or at least Handel himself thought so, and he should know — and was a competent teacher. In any case, Handel never lost respect for his teacher, and after Zachau died in 1712 the now-famous composer regularly sent cash to help out Zachau's widow. Such a *nice* boy.

Zachau taught the boy how to play the organ and harpsichord, a little bit of violin, oboe and a few other instruments, as well as the rudiments of theory, composition and performance practice. Handel was such a fast learner that within just a few years he was able to substitute for Zachau on the organ for church services at the *Liebfrauenkirche* from time to time. [7]

The young Handel also began composing his own music, which he did by following the accepted practice of his day. First he copied out other composers' music, to get a feel for it, and then he would try to imitate it. (In later years, as we'll discover, Handel sometimes took this habit of copying to extremes.)

Both in copying and composing his own music, Zachau

---

[7] J.S. Bach tried out for the *Liebfrauenkriche* organist's job after Zachau's death. But the pay wasn't so good, so he took a gig at Weimar instead. A few years later, the job went to Wilhelm Friedemann Bach, one of old J.S.'s many sons.

kept Handel busy scribbling away, requiring him to compose a new church cantata each week, and lots more besides. "I used to write like the devil in those days," Handel later told Charles Burney, the noted English busybody.

Especially in those early years, biographer Paul Henry Lang tells us, much of Handel's music was written "rather loosely, and with a careless hand." Whatever else Zachau was teaching him, it certainly wasn't penmanship.

Handel studied with Zachau until he was 11 years old. Then, in 1696, maybe as a reward for his hard work and maybe to give him a chance to perform a little himself, he was allowed to travel to Berlin to hang around with some really good professional musicians.

Berlin was bustling in those days, a busy, cosmopolitan capital city presided over by Friedrich III, Elector of Brandenburg. Friedrich, who later became Friedrich I, King of Prussia, loved music and opera and theatre and generally being a downright rich and cultured guy. But mostly he just loved showing off. Friedrich had, as one historian puts it, "a boundless taste for picturesque profligacy." So there.

Friedrich's second wife, Sophia Charlotte, by the way, was the daughter of the Elector of Hanover and the sister of Georg Ludwig, who later became King George I of England and therefore Handel's boss by the time he wrote *Messiah*. [8]

Sophia Charlotte, something of a musical dilettante herself, was pretty impressed when she and the Elector had a chance to hear the young Handel play. Impressed enough

---

[8] It was a small world in those days, especially if you were a member of European royalty.

that she got the Elector to write to Handel's father, offering the boy a position at court, complete with further musical training in Italy.

It was a generous offer, but old Handel would have none of it. He ordered his son to return to Halle immediately. He still wanted a lawyer in the family. (Maybe Georg was just trying to save himself some money. Hiring lawyers was expensive, even back then.)

Handel's father died in 1697, but the dutiful son continued his studies and enrolled at the University of Halle in 1702, at the age of 17. He fully intended to study law and become a lawyer. He really did.

But you know how it is, something came up. What came up was the chance of a job as an organist at the Halle *Schlosskirche,* or *Domkirche,* the Calvinist cathedral. Handel got the job, even though he was a Lutheran, which made some of the Calvinist church elders a bit nervous. But even though Handel was very young and belonged to the wrong church, they probably figured they couldn't do worse than his predecessor, Johann Christoph Leporin. They'd had to fire Leporin for showing up drunk once too often one Sunday morning.

Handel's job at the *Domkirche* paid 50 thalers a year and came with its own apartment. In one of the earliest of his many canny financial moves, Handel continued to live at home and sublet the apartment for another 16 thalers a year. He always was a wheeler-dealer. [9]

[9] This little anecdote would probably be more meaningful if we had a clear sense of how much a thaler was worth in today's money. I wish I could help you there. Anyway, 50 of them was considered an OK salary for a church organist.

After only a year at the church gig, the young Handel decided he needed new challenges and the chance to seek fame and fortune in the big city. So he decided to move to Hamburg to become an opera composer. Or, as Richard A. Streatfeild's biography puts it, "Pegasus burst from his harness, and sought the viewless fields of air." Like I said, he moved to Hamburg.

After Handel left the *Domkirche*, the gig went to Johann Kohlhart. I'm not sure who has it now.

You may be wondering what all of this has to do with *Messiah*, but don't worry, we'll get there.

It was in Hamburg that Handel became friends with Johann Mattheson, an opera singer, fellow composer and amateur music historian a few years older than he was. Mattheson, who knew the ropes of his home town, helped Handel get a job playing second violin in the pit orchestra of the Hamburg opera house. It was one of the few times in his life that Handel put up with playing second fiddle for anybody.

By and large, the two composers got on quite well, although both being the temperamental type, their friendship was not without its rough spots, including a little professional jealousy. (Mattheson thought Handel wrote "really interminable cantatas." Handel doesn't say what he thought of Mattheson's.) [10]

Their most infamous quarrel came on December 5, 1704, during a performance of Mattheson's opera *Cleopatra*, in which the composer himself conducted the orchestra and

[10] If he were looking for a cheap shot, Handel had plenty of ammunition. During the first ten years of his opera career, Mattheson sang mostly female roles.

also sang the role of Anthony, zipping onto the stage whenever necessary and leaving Handel to fill in on the harpsichord in his absence. Since Anthony dies about half an hour from the end, Mattheson liked to return to the orchestra pit for the last part of the show, picking up the harpsichord part again and of course taking all the bows and curtain calls.

On the night in question, it seems Handel decided he didn't want to give up his place at the harpsichord and let Mattheson steal all the glory (although it *was* his opera, after all), whereupon Mattheson, more than a little miffed, called him a variety of rude names and challenged him to step outside to settle the matter in a duel.

That might have been the end of young Handel, who was no particular star as a swordsman (Wagner was much better in the duelling department).[11] In which case we'd have no *Messiah* to worry about, and no reason to continue on with this book. But as luck would have it, scarcely had the two drawn weapons and lunged when Mattheson's sword struck a brass button on Handel's coat and snapped off. They took it as a sign (of good tailoring, if nothing else), forgot their quarrel and decided to remain friends. This just goes to show that your mother was right. You should always make sure all your buttons are sewn on properly. Neatness *does* count. [12]

[11] Duelling had been outlawed at the University of Halle shortly after Handel enrolled there, so he was dangerously out of practice.

[12] There's something a little eerie about all this. Handel's life is saved by a well-sewn button, Palestrina made his fortune in the fur and leather garment trade, Brahms's mother was a seamstress. Maybe counterpoint and needlepoint aren't all that dissimilar after all. Maybe there's a pattern here, or at least the thread of an idea.

A single brass button can be a real life saver

Handel had a few of his operas produced in Hamburg before moving on to Italy in 1706, where he schmoozed the local Italian musical crowd and wrote a few more operas, just to keep in shape. He also composed a *Te Deum*, the church anthem *Dixit Dominus* and a number of Italian love duets. [13]

Some Handel writers believe that it was during this visit to Rome that winter that he had a chance to hear the shepherds of the Abruzzi region, called the *pifferari*, who come down from their mountain pastures at Christmas time to "play their quaint bagpipe melodies in the streets of Rome," as Streatfeild puts it. (I'm not sure that "quaint" and "bagpipe" are two words that can usually be used in the same sentence. But these are very small bagpipes, so they're not quite as noisy as their Scottish counterparts.)

At any rate, goes the theory, the title *Pifa* that appears in *Messiah* for the *Pastoral Symphony* orchestral interlude in Part I was either based on or inspired by one of these little shepherd tunes.

This would seem to make sense, since it serves to introduce the soprano recitative about the shepherds abiding in the field, and washing their socks by night, or however it goes. The sound of the bagpipe drone is even there in the pedal C of the opening few bars and the pedal G in bar 13, for example. (For a while after the battle of Culloden Moor, wearing kilts and playing bagpipes were expressly forbidden. But this only worked for a while. You can't stop people

[13] Don't forget about those. They'll show up later

from playing the bagpipes, however hard you might try.)[14]

From Italy, Handel moved back to Germany in 1711, to take the job of *Kapellmeister*, or court composer, to Georg Ludwig, the Elector of Hanover. The job paid him 1,000 thalers a year, a darn sight better than the 50 thalers he'd been making as a church organist in Halle only seven years before. Handel had hit the big time.

He'd hardly begun the job when he managed to get a leave of absence to visit England, where he spent about seven months composing operas (or reworking his old ones, since the English audiences had never heard them and wouldn't know the difference) and generally having a good time doing his Famous Composer routine.

He returned to Germany briefly, but only long enough to convince his boss to let him go back to England, "on condition that he engaged to return within a reasonable time," Mainwaring's biography tells us. Considering that this second London "visit" lasted nearly 50 years, until his death in 1759, I'm not sure that could be considered "reasonable." But his promise to the Elector, Mainwaring says, just "somehow slipt out of his memory." You know how it is.

It hardly mattered anyway, since in 1714 Georg Ludwig the Elector of Hanover became King George I of England, and therefore remained Handel's boss whether he liked it or not.

---

[14] An old story goes that a mother once asked playwright and music critic George Bernard Shaw what instrument her son might take up that would save her the agony of having to put up with those early stages when he couldn't play it very well. Shaw, being witty but not very helpful, suggested the bagpipes, on the theory that they sound no worse at the beginning than when you've been playing them for years and years.

Between 1714 and 1830, every king of England was named George. They were all members of the House of Hanover, which is in Germany. It rather embarrassed the English to have to import their royal family from Germany, but they didn't have much choice. They'd more or less run out of Stuarts. (Well, not entirely, but that's another story.) Anyway, the first four Hanoverians were all called George. To make them easier to tell apart, they were numbered, with typical Germanic efficiency, George I, George II, George III and George IV.

George I could hardly speak English, so he spent a lot of time standing around wondering what everyone was saying. His son, George II, learned a bit more English and got involved in the Battle of Jenkins's Ear.

This little war really did start, believe it or not, because of someone's ear. [15] It seems that Robert Jenkins, who was a sailor (well, a pirate, actually) got into a bit of a scuffle with some Spaniards, and one of them cut off his ear. At this point, Jenkins said, thinking they were about to kill him, "I commended my soul to my God, and my cause to my country," thereby in one fell swoop starting a war and neatly ensuring his place in all those quotation dictionaries. Jenkins used to carry his ear around in a little box. He'd show it to you, if you asked him nicely. [16]

---

[15] Jenkins's ear, in fact.

[16] Never mind that the thing in the box might not have been his ear at all, or that he might actually have lost it in a bar fight. The incident was enough to send England to war with Spain. It was just the sort of excuse the English were looking for. They hadn't had a good war with Spain since they'd trounced the Spanish Armada back in 1588.

Despite being such a big war hero, with all sorts of medals he'd awarded himself, George II's death was less than glorious. Always one to suffer constipation, George II had a heart attack while sitting on the toilet. The strain had been too much for him.

George II's grandson, George III, went a little bonkers, started talking to trees and misplaced the American colonies. George IV mostly stayed out of the way and let his wife, Caroline of Anspach, run things. She was so much better at it.

There was a gap there for a while, and then there were a couple more Georges. The position of George VII is still vacant, if you're interested and you know the right people.

But I digress. Handel's chief rival as an opera composer in the 1720s was Giovanni Bononcini, an Italian composer who had come to London in 1719. Some of their followers took this rivalry quite seriously, while others failed to see what all the fuss was about.

One of these was the wag John Byrom, who when he wasn't thinking up clever things to say had invented a new form of shorthand. (Sometimes those witty sayings would pop into his head and he'd just have to get them down on paper before he forgot.) He dined out more than once on the strength of this humorous little ditty:

> Some say, compar'd to Bononcini,
> That Mynheer Handel's but a Ninny;
> Others aver that he to Handel
> Is scarcely fit to hold a Candle:
> Strange, all this difference should be
> 'Twixt Tweedledum and Tweedledee

This little poem is sometimes attributed to Jonathan Swift, but Byrom deserves the credit. Around 1780, Pieter Hellendaal set it to music and it made the rounds as a glee. (Mynheer, by the way, is the Dutch form of Mister. Byrom obviously got confused between Dutch and Deustch, or German. This is generally not a wise thing to do.)[17]

Although Handel enjoyed considerable success at first composing operas for the London scene, after a while the novelty began to wear off. Operas were difficult to compose, expensive to produce, and you were always having to deal with temperamental opera stars.

Besides, as the years went on and audiences became more fickle, there was no longer any guarantee that any new opera would make the composer a lot of money. (Handel twice had to declare bankruptcy and was almost constantly concerned about money. It didn't help matters that on the second night of his opera *Teseo*, in January 1713, theatre manager Owen Swiney — a.k.a. Owen MacSwiney — skipped town with the box-office receipts. After that, Handel got himself a more trustworthy theatre manager, named Johann Jacob Heidegger.)

The success in 1728 of the ballad-opera *The Beggar's Opera,* by Johann Pepusch and John Gay, put another nail in the coffin of Handel's opera career. Audiences liked ballad-operas because they were sung in English, so they could understand the words, and the tunes were immediately recognizable, having been stolen from all over the place.

---

[17] Handel got his revenge on his Italian rival later on. The chorus *Sion now her head shall raise,* from *Judas Maccabeus* and quite possibly the last thing Handel ever wrote, is based on a tune he stole from Bononcini in 1758.

(Including, to add insult to injury, from Handel himself.) It was about this time that Handel began thinking that maybe he'd just give up on this whole opera deal altogether. [18]

As early as 1732, Handel began experimenting with composing oratorios, which tell a dramatic story in musical form just like opera, but without the added trouble of all those expensive sets and costumes.

"It is interesting to speculate," says musicologist John Tobin, "what Handel oratorio owes to Cavalieri's *La rappresentatione di Anima e Corpo* [or to] Monteverdi's *Combattimento di Tancredi e Clorinda*," not to mention (as Tobin, in fact, does) Schütz's *Historia von der Geburt Gottes und Mariens Sohn Jesu Christe* or even Carissimi's *Jephthe*.

Yes, it would be interesting. Let me know how it turns out.

Handel's first oratorio was *Esther*, followed closely by *Deborah*, then later *Saul and Israel in Egypt*. [19]

But none of these has attained the popularity of *Messiah*, which Handel composed in a hurry for some quick cash, little suspecting that it would become such a big hit.

Interestingly enough, Handel did not consider *Messiah* to be his best oratorio, despite its overwhelming popularity. This honor he reserved for *Theodora*, an oratorio he wrote years later and which hardly anyone has heard of, much less heard.

---

[18] He might have been tempted by the example of English composer John Eccles — who, like Handel, based his opera *Semele* on a libretto provided by William Congreve. Eccles, once the Master of the King's Musick, retired early and spent the rest of his life fishing.

[19] *Esther* was a bit of a cheat, actually, since all Handel did was rework his earlier opera *Haman and Moredecai*.

In fact, Handel thought that *He saw the lovely youth*, one of the choruses from *Theodora*, was the best one he ever wrote, better even than the *Hallelujah* chorus. This just goes to show that creators are not always the best judges of their own popularity. [20]

But the first performance of *Theodora* at Covent Garden, on March 16, 1750, was not a rousing success. In fact, it went so badly that Handel went home and angrily tore up the score. (Somebody put it back together again later on.)

Critics suggest several reasons why *Theodora* never caught on with audiences. For one thing, it doesn't have a happy ending. Both Theodora and her lover, Didimus, die in the end, which tends to put audiences in a bad mood. And Theodora, although heroic and brave, is not exactly as virtuous as prudish audiences seemed to expect of their heroines. (As Winton Dean so coyly puts it in his book on Handel's oratorios, she does not "wear the robes of formalized virginity.")

You'll notice that most Handel oratorios — *Esther*, *Deborah*, and the rest — are based on Old Testament stories. In fact, *Theodora* is the only English oratorio besides *Messiah* to be based on a Christian theme. [21] Yet even that wasn't enough to ensure its success. There's just no pleasing some people.

---

[20] Sir Arthur Conan Doyle, who created Sherlock Holmes, was convinced that he'd be remembered for *The White Company, Sir Nigel* and his other stuffy historical novels. He was wrong there.

[21] Yes, I know there's Mendelssohn's *St. Paul*. But he wrote that in German, so it doesn't count.

CHAPTER 4

OFF TO DUBLIN FOR THE GREEN

When Irish ears are buying

OFF TO DUBLIN
FOR THE GREEN

I F 1741 HAD BEEN A BETTER year for Handel, he might not have had any reason to accept an invitation to leave London for a musical visit to Dublin. As it was, he was grateful for any excuse to get out of town.

The opera season of 1740-41 had not been going at all well for Handel. Miserably, in fact. His opera *Imeneo* had opened and closed after only two performances. *Deidamia*, at least, had managed to last for three. Where once audiences had flocked to see his operas, now they were staying away in droves. [1]

So despite what financial analysts might have called this "slight upward trend" in box-office returns from (three performances is a *little* better than two, after all), Handel was getting pretty discouraged. It was enough to make him chuck opera entirely, which in fact he did after *Deidamia*. Although "real" operas by Handel and others

---

[1] Adding insult to injury — with an irony that would not have been lost on Handel — *Imeneo* had opened on Nov. 22, the feast day of St. Cecilia, the patron saint of music. Even that didn't help.

weren't doing well, *The Beggar's Opera* and other ballad-operas were still packing them in, much the same as such popular musicals as *Cats, Phantom* and *Les Miz* do today. Handel said if that's what they wanted they were welcome to it.

What he really wanted to do was go off to a spa somewhere and soak his feet and drown his sorrows in the hot mineral baths. [2] But when the chance came to go to Ireland, Handel decided to jump at it. After all, what did he have to lose?

The invitation came from William Cavendish, the Duke of Devonshire, a rich but amiable twit whom the King of England had recently appointed Lord Lieutenant of Ireland. [3]

We're not precisely sure what form this invitation took, but Cavendish may simply have said: "I say, Handel, old chap, I think it would be an absolutely *spiffy* idea if you and a few of your musical chappies should come over here to Dublin and put on a little show for me and my hangers-on. Nothing too grand, you know, just an opera or an oratorio or whatnot.

"You've no idea how *frightfully* boring it is out here in the provinces. We miss London terribly, you know. So do

---

[2] Handel liked spas, especially the one at Tunbridge Wells. They were good for his gout.

[3] For a more detailed history of Anglo-Irish relations and their effect on life in Ireland, particularly with respect to Home Rule, political control, power struggles and the influence of English nobility, the serious reader should refer to such works as Geoffrey Keating's *History of Ireland* in four volumes, William E. Lecky's three-volume *History of Ireland in the Eighteenth Century*, or T.A. Jackson's *Ireland Her Own: An Outline History of the Irish Struggle for National Freedom & Independence*. Or just ask anyone who lives there.

come along next month, there's a good fellow, and we shall have a jolly good time, eh what?"

Or words to that effect.

At any rate, Handel set off for Ireland early in November 1741, arriving in Dublin about two weeks later. The journey wouldn't normally have taken quite so long, but Handel decided to make a few stops along the way. (The Lord Lieutenant himself could make the trip in five days, we're told, but then he didn't have to worry about the speed limits.)

Among the delays were the few days Handel spent in Chester, hanging around a tavern called The Golden Falcon. Ostensibly this was because the winds were too strong for a safe crossing over to Ireland. (That's the problem with living on an island: everywhere you look you're surrounded by water.) Or it may have been that The Golden Falcon had particularly good draft on tap.

Whatever the reason, Handel decided to make good use of the time by throwing together a few singers and going over a few little bits of *Messiah*, just to hear how they would sound.

Charles Burney, who went on to become a famous musical Nosy Parker, gossip-monger and general gadabout, tells an amusing anecdote about Handel's little Chester sessions. (I like it so much that I've already mentioned it in my earlier book *Bach, Beethoven, And The Boys: Music History As It Ought To Be Taught*. But hey, if it's good enough for Burney to repeat, it's good enough for me.)

Burney was in Chester when it happened, going to school there. He was only about 15 at the time of Handel's visit, but he believed in being nosy from an early age. It gave him so many more stories to tell when he got older. [4]

It seems that among the singers Handel assembled for the occasion was a printer named Janson, who had been recommended to him as a bass and a good sight-reader. But during a run-through of the chorus *And with his stripes we are healed*, Janson apparently made so many mistakes that Handel shouted at him: "I thought you told me you could read music at sight!"

Janson's reply is a classic. "Yes, sir, and so I can," he told the red-faced composer. "But not at *first* sight." Improve on *that*, would you? [5]

Anyway, Handel's ship docked on the 18th (of November, remember, in case you've lost track), and the Dublin papers were quick to note the arrival of "the celebrated Dr. Handell."

The reference to "Dr." was a sore point with the composer, who never received the degree. Oxford University had offered him an honorary doctorate when he went there in 1733, and Handel was pleased to accept it, until he found out they were going to charge him £100 for the privilege. At which point, he told Oxford to take its degree and go stuff it in its ear. Anyway, pretty soon the Dublin papers learned to call him "Mister," though they never did always spell the "Handel" part properly. (You can never trust newspapers.) [6]

---

[4] Burney's *A General History of Music* runs to four volumes. Feel free to look through it, if you like.

[5] "The authenticity of this anecdote is questionable," Handel historian Donald Burrows announces solemnly. Don't you just hate spoilsports?

[6] Handel didn't need a doctorate. He could already swear, quite colorfully, in at least four modern languages, and probably a couple of dead ones, too.

Handel rented a little house on Abbey Street, got settled in and prepared to launch a new concert season of "Musical Entertainments" for the Dublin audiences.

Apart from *Messiah*, Handel brought several other big works with him to Dublin for the season. These included *Acis and Galatea, Ode for St. Cecilia's Day, Esther, Alexander's Feast*, and the three-section chorus *L'Allegro, il Penseroso, ed il Moderato*. (*L'Allegro* and *il Penseroso* are poems by John Milton. The third part, *il Moderato*, was added by Charles Jennens a year or so before he sent Handel the libretto for *Messiah*.) [7]

To be on the safe side, Handel also brought along a bunch of organ concertos, anthems and other short works, just to fill in the gaps. And he spent a good deal of time improvising on the organ to please the crowds. [8]

[7] Libretto, as you probably already know, is just fancy musicians' talk for "the words," or "the text." It comes from the Italian word meaning "little book," although many of them are anything but little. The person who writes the libretto is called, naturally enough, the librettist — or, in the case of *Messiah*, "Charlie-boy," or "Chuck." The plural of libretto is libretti, if you want to sound all fancy and Italian, or librettos, if you want to sound a little less pretentious. Nowadays, most people would probably just say "lyrics."

[8] "The Musick sounds delightfully in this charming Room," Handel writes in a letter to Jennens in December 1741, "which puts me in such Spirits (and my Health being so good) that I exert myself on my Organ with more than usual Success." I can only assume by "organ" that he means the musical instrument found in churches. Otherwise I wouldn't know *what* to think.

CHAPTER 5

THE FIRST-FRUITS

Packing them in at Neal's Music Hall

THE FIRST-FRUITS

FOR OUR PURPOSES, THE most important of Handel's many Dublin concerts was the first performance of *Messiah*. This took place in Neal's Music Hall on Fishamble Street on April 13, 1742. [1]

Fishamble Street still exists in Dublin today, right where it always was, not far from Christ Church Cathedral, St. Patrick's Cathedral and the River Liffey.

The name, by the way, has nothing to do with fish ambling, or walking slowly, down the street. That would be silly, even for Ireland. Long before Handel's time, it used to be a fish market ("shambles" is the old name for a market stall).

The Music Hall no longer stands, having been torn down years ago to make room for a factory. There's a nice plaque, though, which tourists like to take pictures of.

There's something fitting in the name, of course, considering that so many productions of *Messiah* end up in a shambles anyway.

[1]   Burney was of the opinion that Handel had given a performance of *Messiah* in London before arriving in Dublin. But he was wrong. Burney was wrong about a lot of things, actually.

There had already been a rehearsal open to the public on April 9, which Faulkner's *Dublin Journal* said "was allowed by the greatest Judges to be the finest Composition of Musick that ever was heard." Your basic rave review. The paper also said it was "performed so well, that it gave universal Satisfaction to all present."

Not to be outdone, the *Dublin News-Letter* said of the public rehearsal, "in the opinion of the best Judges [it] far surpasses anything of that Nature which has been performed in this or any other Kingdom." You kind of get the idea they liked it, too. [2]

The first performance was also a rousing success ("Sublime ... Grand ... Tender" — *Dublin Journal*; "exquisite Delight" — *Dublin Gazette*; "elevated, majestick and moving Words" — *Dublin News-Letter*). [3]

About 700 people showed up for the first official performance, which was a bit of a problem, since the concert hall was designed to seat only 600. I imagine things got a little cozy. To make things a little more comfortable for the audience, newspaper advertisements announcing the concert had stated that, in order to make more room, women should wear skirts without hoops and the men should leave their swords at home. It's so much safer that way.

There were no reports of any injuries, so either the gentlemen did remember to leave their swords at home or they were all very careful about not jabbing anyone. I'm not

---

[2] It must have been quite the audience, what with all those Judges hanging around. I wonder if they wore their funny wigs?

[3] The Bishop of Elphin liked *Messiah* so much that he said Handel should follow it with a little something of his own, called *The Penitent*. Handel told him thanks very much and did nothing more about it.

sure about the ladies and their hoop skirts. [4]

It's not true that Handel wrote *Messiah* specifically for its Dublin premiere, although the members of Dublin society liked to think so. [5]

He'd actually written it months earlier, with no particular performance in mind, back home in London. Charles Jennens had sent him the libretto and he liked it, so he set it to music, simple as that. [6]

After Handel finished composing *Messiah*, he put it away in a drawer and immediately set to work composing *Saul*. You never knew when a new oratorio or two might come in handy.

Handel composed *Messiah* in a typical burst of energy between August 22 and September 14, 1741, or the space of just over three weeks. Jennens thought he should have taken more time, and would get a little testy on the subject if you asked him. "He has made a fine entertainment of it," Jennens says in a letter, "though not near so good as he might and ought to have done."

That was fast writing, even for Handel, but by no means a record. He was used to dashing things off in a hurry. Most of his operas and many of his other oratorios

[4] It might be fascinating to try to track down cleaning bills in Dublin at the time, to see whether, in the days following the *Messiah* performances, there was a rush of ladies' skirts being ironed out. (They get a lot more wrinkled if you leave the hoops out, you know.) Oddly enough, to the best of my knowledge no enterprising Handel scholar has done anything to look into this. (Not even Otto Erich Deutsch, and his book includes just about everything *but* laundry lists.) I'd love to help out, but I really don't have time. Sorry.

[5] And Handel didn't tell them otherwise. He didn't want to spoil their fun.

[6] Well, simple if you're Handel, maybe.

were written in the space of a few weeks or months. But he must have cared more for *Messiah* than those others, because he spent more time tinkering with it afterwards to get it just right. (This must have made Jennens feel at least a little better.)

Since he wrote it in such a hurry, Handel took many of his usual shortcuts in the notation, which later led to a little confusion. Sometimes he got the words wrong, too. But considering the rush, it's perhaps surprising that, for *Messiah*, Handel doesn't seem to have stolen any of the music from anyone but himself, and then only for a few movements.

This shows admirable restraint, especially when you consider his track record. Large parts of *Theodora*, for instance, seem to have come from the Italian composer Giovanni Carlo Maria Clari, an entire movement from Gottlieb Muffat's *Componimenti*, and a few bits from Bononcini's *Griselda*. Parts of *Israel in Egypt* are based on a *Magnificat* by Dionigi Erba. For some of his other works, Handel also borrowed bits here and there from Johann Habermann, Karl Heinrich Graun, Alessandro Stradella and a few others, I'm sure. [7]

But it seems that almost all of the music for *Messiah* was brand spanking new, except for a few little choruses that are based on the music Handel wrote a few years earlier for some Italian love duets. [8]

For example, *And he shall purify* comes from *L'occaso ha nell'aurora*, while *For unto us a child is born* comes from the duet *No di voi non vo'fidarmi* and he used a few most of the others for *His yoke is easy, All we like sheep*

[7] Oh yes, and Johann Kerll, too.
[8] See, I told you they'd show up again.

and *O Death, where is thy sting?* and the chorus that follows it, *But thanks be to God.*

Knowing this helps make some sense of some of these choruses. I've always wondered, for instance, why in *His yoke* the sixteenth-note runs always land on the word "easy," which makes it very difficult to sing. (The chorus should really be called "His yoke is anything *but* easy.") But in the original Italian duet, the runs land on the word *ride*, the Italian word for "laugh." Listen to it again, and you'll find that the running bits really do suggest laughter more than anything else. Certainly not "easy."

Anyway, Sedley Taylor, who in 1906 wrote an entire book on the subject of Handel's "borrowings," is obviously pleased that the composer kept such impulses in check when writing *Messiah.*

"One would fain hope," Taylor intones, "that this immunity is inherent in that sublime work by the deliberate will of the composer." Or maybe he just couldn't remember anything else he wanted to steal.

Handel brought a couple of singers with him as soloists for his Dublin season, including the soprano Christina Maria Avoglio and the contralto Susannah Cibber. Avoglio had sung in some Handel operas in London, while Cibber had sung in his oratorio *Deborah.* Both of them sang in the *Messiah* debut.

Although Cibber was known primarily as an actress in stage comedies, she had done her share of singing. Ironically, her most successful role to date had been as Polly Peachum in *The Beggar's Opera*, the very work that had driven Handel to take up oratorio. Now here she was about to star in his most important one.

Funny how life works out that way.

By all accounts, Susannah Cibber was not a great musician. Her voice was small and she could hardly read music. She had to learn everything by rote, and apparently Handel spent hours going over and over her part with her until she had it down pat. [9]

Susannah Cibber had long dark curly hair and big brown eyes and lovely pale skin and a nose rather large for the rest of her face. She once boasted that it took her three hours to get her hair ready. I'm surprised she found time for anything else.

She was considered quite pretty, yes, but pretty's not enough, especially for singing oratorio. She may not have had a fabulous and well-trained voice (Burney says it was just "a thread") but what she did have, and the reason Handel was happy to have her in his cast, was a terrific dramatic sense and the ability to deliver emotion. When she sang something poignant, there wasn't a dry eye in the house.

Handel said he composed the alto solo aria *He was despised* specifically with her voice in mind (and he said writing it had made him a little weepy, too). He also transposed *If God be for us* and the second part of *He shall feed his flock,* originally set for soprano, so she could sing them.

In fact, Cibber's delivery was so moving that, as the story goes, at the first performance after she had finished singing *He was despised*, Dr. Patrick Delany, the chancellor

---

[9] Don't worry, biographer Newman Flower assures us that the relationship between Handel and Cibber was nothing more than "a great and clean friendship." Well, *that's* a relief.

of St. Patrick's Cathedral, stood up from the audience and shouted, "Woman, for this, be all thy sins forgiven."

That was awfully decent of him, especially considering that Susannah Cibber had more than a few sins that probably needed forgiving. In fact, her escapades had made her quite the talk of the town.

Her father was Thomas Arne, an upholsterer and coffin-maker from a long line of upholsterers and coffin-makers. In 1710, he had played host to four Iroquois chiefs who were on a state visit to London to meet Queen Anne. [10]

If the British had thought of them as real royalty, the chiefs would probably have stayed at one of the many royal palaces. But as it was, they stayed at Arne's place, which at least was more comfortable than they were used to back home. [11]

Apparently, the Iroquois chiefs found the upholstery at The Two Crowns and Cushions (that was the name of Arne's shop) so comfortable they gave him the honorary title "Cataraqui," after their settlement where Kingston, Ontario, Canada now stands. [12]

Thomas Arne and his wife Anne had two children: Thomas Augustine, or Tom Jr., and Susannah.

Thomas Augustine Arne is another one of those composers whose father, Tom Sr., wanted him to become a lawyer. T.A. Arne became a famous composer anyway. Among other things, he composed a masque (a sort of mini-opera) called

---

[10] Oh, you know, the one with all the chairs. And the lace.

[11] I'm not sure how you say "I'm off to London to visit the Queen" in Iroquois, but that's probably what they told everybody.

[12] And where I lived for many years. Small world, isn't it?

Alfred, from which we get the song *Rule, Britannia*.

In 1734, Susannah Arne married Theophilus Cibber, an actor-manager at the Drury Lane Theatre and a bit of a cad. [13]

While still married to Theo, Susannah met William Sloper, who was handsome and very rich and spent most of his time hanging around the tennis courts. I guess he looked good in white. He had a wife named Catherine, but that didn't seem to get in the way of his becoming good friends with Susannah Cibber. [14]

Theo was less than pleased, though perhaps he had only himself to blame. He had introduced them, after all.[15]

In fact, Theo went so far as to take Sloper to court and sue him for £5,000, since he had witnesses to testify that the affair had been going on. The main witness was a man named Hayes, who with his wife had rented rooms for a little "love nest" where Susannah Cibber and William Sloper could meet.

How did Hayes know all this? Simple. Theo had paid him to sit in a closet and watch them through a hole he'd drilled in the wainscotting. Sometimes he'd watch them for

---

[13] Susannah was no fool. She had made Theo sign a pre-nuptial agreement preventing him from getting his hands on her acting salary. That's quite an accomplishment for those days, when a husband usually had complete control over the family money. But you didn't want Theo controlling your money if you could help it.

[14] Their daughter was born in February 1740 and they named her Maria Susannah, or Susannah Maria — or Molly because they could never agree on the right order. She was, you might say, the first-fruits of them that slept together.

[15] And he was, let's face it, not exactly Mr. Virtuous himself.

hours at a time. (He was merely being thorough, you understand.) [16]

Theophilus Cibber won his lawsuit against William Sloper, but it was hardly the money-making victory he had hoped for. Instead of £5,000, the jury awarded him only £10, which wouldn't even cover his legal costs. Theo tried again several months later, this time suing Sloper for £10,000. That jury awarded him £500. Well, at least he was getting somewhere.

Anyway, it was to get away from her husband and all the publicity of the trials that Susannah Cibber was glad to escape to Dublin and take work in the theatres there, and also to perform in Handel's new oratorio.

The other soloists for that first performance of *Messiah* were not nearly so notorious. In fact, downright dull.

There was another soprano, "Mrs. Maclaine," or "MacLean," who was the wife of the organist; there were two counter-tenors, Joseph Lambe and Michael Ward; a tenor, James Bailey; and a bass, John Mason. (The *Dublin Journal* lists the counter-tenor soloists as William Lamb and Joseph Ward, and includes John Church as another tenor soloist and John Hill as another bass. As I said before, you can't trust newspapers.)

The chorus consisted of 32 singers — 16 boy trebles and 16 men for the other parts — drawn from the choirs of

[16] Although the judge had ordered a publication ban on the trial, someone must have secretly been taking notes. An enterprising bookseller named Trott soon published a 30-page pamphlet recounting Hayes's testimony in all its salacious detail. The Harvard law library has a copy, if you care to read it. It's pretty racy stuff.

Dublin's two cathedrals, Christ Church and St. Patrick's. The orchestra, led by violinist Matthew Dubourg, a longtime friend of Handel's, was quite small, also numbering about 32 players. [17]

I'm not certain whether it was for the *Messiah* debut or for one of the other Dublin concerts, but good old Burney tells a funny little story about Dubourg. It seems that for one of the concert pieces, Dubourg had an extended violin cadenza. This cadenza went on so long, and Dubourg got himself into such remote keys, that it looked like he might have a hard time finishing the thing off. But he eventually modulated back to the right key, at which point Handel said (quite loudly, so everyone in the audience could hear) "You are welcome home, Mr. Dubourg!" He was always such a kidder.

Handel almost didn't have enough singers for that first performance because of a misunderstanding involving St. Patrick's Cathedral. The Dean of St. Patrick's was Jonathan Swift, who earlier in life had found time between sermons to write such popular satires as *Gulliver's Travels* and *A Tale of a Tub.*

Swift was a celebrated writer and a respected member of the clergy who was renowned as a learned scholar. By the time he was just three years old, we're told, he could read any part of the Bible. At university, he was fined several times for not going to chapel regularly, but that didn't stop

[17] A man named Ralph Roseingrave was the organist at both cathedrals. I'm not sure how he did it. They must have held church services at different times of the day. At any rate, he was pretty busy on Sundays.

him from eventually landing the top job at one of the most important churches in Ireland. [18]

But by 1742, three years before his death, Dean Swift was in fact not so swift. (He was a few collects shy of a full prayer book, if you catch my drift.) He was moody, irritable, forgetful and generally not a pleasant fellow anymore. [19]

Anyway, having originally agreed to allow the members of the choir, known as vicars-choral, to sing in Handel's new work, Swift promptly turned around and claimed he'd done nothing of the kind.

He even wrote an angry letter to the sub-dean, strongly objecting to the performance involving "a club of fiddlers at Fishamble Street." He ordered the sub-dean to "punish such vicars as shall ever appear there, as songsters, fiddlers, pipers, trumpeters, drummers, drum-majors, or in any sonal quality, according to the flagitious aggravations of their respective disobedience, rebellion, perfidy, and ingratitude." (Boy, when Swift dashed off a memo, he really meant it.) [20]

Anyway, someone — probably Dr. Delany who liked Susannah Cibber's singing so much — managed to placate old Swift and the performance went ahead as scheduled.

The first performance of *Messiah* was a charity event, held to raise money "For Relief of the Prisoners of the several Gaols, and for the Support of Mercer's Hospital in Stephen's Street, and of the Charitable Infirmary on the Inns

[18] It didn't hurt that Swift knew some of the right people.

[19] Personally, I attribute at least some of Swift's mental deterioration to the fact that, throughout his life, he obstinately refused to wear glasses, even though he'd needed them for a long time.

[20] "Flagitious" is not a word that comes up very often anymore in casual conversation. My dictionary defines it as "shamefully wicked."

Quay." In a spirit of generosity, Handel and the principal performers waived their usual fees. Wasn't that good of them?

The first performance took in £400, of which £127, after expenses, went to each of the three charitable groups (the jails and the two hospitals). There was another performance on June 3 (with a rehearsal on June 1), also at the Fishamble Street concert hall. In order to make things more comfortable for both audience and performers in the summer heat, a pane of glass was removed from the top of each window to improve the air circulation. That helped, but not much.

The June performances aren't listed as fundraisers, so presumably Handel actually got to see some money from those ones. But donating his fee from the premiere was typical of Handel, who was always generous to charities. Years before, he had helped establish a fund "For the Support of Decay'd Musicians and their Families" in London. He continued to contribute money, and compose new works for its efforts, throughout his life. [21]

After returning to London, Handel gave many performances of *Messiah* to help raise money for the Foundling Hospital, of which he became a major benefactor.

But we're getting ahead of ourselves. We should spend a bit more time looking at the creation of *Messiah*, especially the story behind the creation of the libretto. It's quite a tale.

---

[21] He must have known that he'd become a decayed musician himself one day.

CHAPTER 6

IN THE BEGINNING WERE THE WORDS

A little divine inspiration

IN THE BEGINNING
WERE THE WORDS

S INCE THE WORDS FORM such an important part
of what makes *Messiah* so effective, it's only right
that we take a look at where they came from. After all, there
must be *something* special about them, or else choral societies all over the world might be putting on productions of
Theodora every Christmas.

Messiah doesn't actually tell a story, at least not in the
usual narrative sense of oratorios, which came out of the
dramatic opera tradition. Instead, it is a carefully assembled
compilation of Scriptural verses from the Bible, using both
the Old and New Testaments. (Sometimes, as is the case
with *I know that my Redeemer liveth*, it cleverly combines
both Old and New Testaments in one movement.) While the
libretto doesn't precisely tell a straightforward story, it does
provide a framework for reflection on the life of Christ and
the importance of the Christian message. This has made it
the darling of churches and religious groups everywhere —
although this was not always the case.

Handel was given the libretto for *Messiah* sometime in
the summer of 1741 by Charles Jennens, who also wrote

the librettos for *Saul, L'Allegro, il Penseroso ed il Moderato, Belshazzar*, and quite possibly *Israel in Egypt*.

There seems to be some confusion about this, mostly because some people aren't willing to give credit where it's due.

A diarist named Hone says Jennens collaborated with another man, named Pooley, whom Hone says was a curate and secretary to Jennens. Where he got this I've no idea, since there seems to be no record of anyone named Pooley having anything to do with Jennens at all. Some scholars have suggested Hone must be referring to Matthew Poole, the author of an important book of biblical scholarship. This theory would hold a lot more water if Poole hadn't died in Holland more than half a century earlier, in 1679. [1]

Someone else said Jennens must have collaborated with one of his neighbors, Dr. Bentley of Nailstone. But nobody (except maybe in the Bentley family) takes this one seriously.

Some historians have even suggested that Handel himself created the libretto, in a fit of devotional inspiration after the death of his beloved sister, whose favorite scriptural passage was said to be "I know that my Redeemer liveth." I don't think so. Handel knew his Bible, but not well enough to produce such a well-wrought libretto as this one.

Why make things difficult? I say Charles Jennens wrote the thing and that's the end of it. Let the man bask in his moment of reflected glory. Where's the harm in that?

Much of the problem about Jennens is really the fault of George Steevens, his literary rival, whose attacks on Jennens one scholar has said are nothing short of "character

---

[1] There's always something, isn't there?

assassination." There's no doubt about it, Jennens was a bit of a character, all right.

The Jennens family had managed to amass quite a fortune by the time little Charlie came along in 1700. One of his uncles was a "gentleman of the bedchamber" to William III, but most of the family money came from iron. [2]

Jennens once told a friend that he had been "born and bred in Leicestershire mud," but he was just being modest. Most of the time, he was quite clean and presentable.

Although it was spelled Jennens, the family apparently pronounced its name "Jennings," just to confuse people. (These were the type, after all, who pronounced Leicester as "Lester" and Gloucester as "Gloster." Sometimes I think the English don't know how to pronounce their own language.)

When he was grown up, Jennens spent his winters in London going to the theatres and concert halls, and his summers at the family estate in Leicestershire, called Gopsall. It was a little chunk of property, only 736 acres or so, with a small mansion tucked in among the trees.

His father died in 1747 and Jennens inherited the whole kit and caboodle, including 34 properties in six counties and the nice Gopsall house he liked to call home. [3]

He spent the next 20 years renovating and expanding the house, turning it into a splendid Palladian mansion, which the Royal Institute of British Architects called one of the finest examples of the English Palladian style. Somebody tore it down in 1951 anyway.

[2] I'm not quite sure what a "gentleman of the bedchamber" does. Maybe it's better not to ask.

[3] That's Gopsall, not Gospel, which is something else again.

After he'd finished on the house, Jennens spent a bunch of money on the gardens, turning them into a display area for charming *chinoiserie* temples and bridges. When something didn't look quite right, he'd add a few more bridges until it did.

Since he still had some money left over, Jennens started collecting paintings, until he had 500 or more. When he ran out of wall space, he'd just build another wing on the house to hang them in. What the heck, he had 736 acres to play with. And zoning regulations were much more lax back then.

He also spent a fair amount of time writing letters to his friend Edward Holdsworth, and giving him money to support his research into the works of Virgil. Virgil scholars were having an ongoing battle about the location of Philippi, which Virgil seems to have misplaced somehow. Holdsworth felt that if he'd just re-read Virgil often enough the right answer would come to him. It never did. (Maybe he should have looked at a map.)

Jennens was something of a scholar himself, having set himself the task of editing the complete works of Shakespeare. He managed five volumes before he died in 1773, producing editions of *King Lear, Macbeth, Hamlet, Othello* and *Julius Caesar.*

It was this that brought on the attacks by George Steevens, who called Jennens a fop and a dilettante and a variety of other names it might be best not to repeat. But Steevens was just jealous, plain and simple, because Jennens's Shakespeare work was every bit as good as his own, if not better.

So now I'm not sure whose side to believe. There are

stories that Jennens used to make a big production of travelling through London in a coach and four horses, with footmen to help him to and from the carriage and to sweep the street before and after his passage, that he wore extravagant clothes and foolish wigs and took too much snuff and generally lorded it over the underlings.

On the other hand, it may be that all of these stories came from Steevens and not one of them is true. Just because they've made it into *The Dictionary of National Biography* doesn't mean they're the Gospel (or Gopsall) truth, I suppose.

Although Steevens's attacks on Jennens were quite personal and underhanded, Jennens himself remained the soul of tact (at least in public) and only ever responded with arguments of a scholarly or literary nature. He therefore wins the Good Sportsmanship Award. [4]

Part of the reason Jennens had so much time to edit Shakespeare and write librettos (aside from having servants to do everything else for him) was that he was a member of a special class in British society of the 18th century known as "nonjurors." Nonjurors were members of the upper class who refused to accept the legitimacy of the house of Hanover's claim to the throne, and remained loyal to the deposed house of Stuart. Since nonjurors refused to swear allegiance to the current royal family, this put them in a kind of limbo where they were not allowed to serve as Members of Parliament or magistrates or in various other official positions.

---

[4] If Jennens had wanted to find something underhanded, he needn't have looked very far. Although Steevens had gone to King's College, Cambridge, he never did actually get a degree.

Nonjurors had to be a little careful what they said in public, but as long as they kept a low profile, the government pretty much left them alone.

This could be awkward occasionally, but it did leave them with rather a lot more free time. Jennens used his to write poetry, compile librettos, edit Shakespeare and cross out the names of the Hanoverian kings in all the prayer books in the chapel of his house at Gopsall. Then he felt better. [5]

When in London, Jennens lived in a couple of different houses, one in Queen Square and the other on Great Ormond Street. That area of town was an absolute hotbed of nonjurors, so he fit right in.

In Queen Square, Jennens lived just a couple of houses down from the Bowdler family, and one of his cousins later married one of the Bowdler boys. This is the family that later produced Thomas Bowdler (1754-1825), who became famous for taking all the dirty words (or the words *he* thought were dirty, anyway) out of Shakespeare, thus producing the first "bowdlerized" version, which he called *The Family Shakespeare*.

There's a certain irony here, of course. Jennens spent a good deal of his life editing Shakespeare so all the words would be right, and his distant cousin by marriage later set about to take them all out again. You just can't win sometimes. [6]

Like Handel, Jennens never married. He was a shy man,

---

[5] It was his chapel and they were his books, and if he wanted to write in them, who was going to stop him?

[6] When he was through with Shakespeare, Bowdler tackled Gibbon and took all the dirty parts out of *The Decline and Fall of the Roman Empire*. He got it done, but the effort killed him.

and sometimes got quite miserable, especially when he'd run out of Hanoverians to delete from the prayer books.

Jennens was occasionally rude to Handel behind his back, but mostly in a sort of affectionate way. (His favorite nickname for the composer was "the Prodigious.") Handel was always polite to him in his letters and let him know how the performances were going. [7]

By all accounts, he and Handel got on quite well, all in all. Just a couple of old bachelors spending time with their books and their music. [8]

---

[7] Handel always referred to the Jennens libretto as "your *Messiah*," which ought to put an end to the argument of authorship, I think. Handel wasn't one to let others get the credit unnecessarily.

[8] Jennens bought a harpsichord once, and had it shipped all the way from Florence, but he wasn't happy with it. Later on, Handel advised him on the installation of an organ for the chapel back home.

CHAPTER 7

WELL, HERE'S ANOTHER FINE MESSIAH YOU'VE GOTTEN US INTO

The King's sleepy foot stands on ceremony

WELL, HERE'S
ANOTHER FINE MESSIAH
YOU'VE GOTTEN US INTO

WHEN HANDEL LEFT Dublin in August of 1742 to return to London, he was in a much better mood.[1] The concerts had gone very well, he was once again the musical toast of the town and he even had a little bit of money in his pocket. What could be better?

Almost immediately, he launched into plans for another season, this time with oratorio instead of opera.[2] He revised *Samson* and wrote a new organ concerto for a concert in February of the following year.

Handel also now had new allies on the musical scene. The aristocracy and other mucky-mucks were still hanging around the opera houses, but the increasing (and increasingly richer) middle class was happy to come hear Handel's oratorios. And Handel wasn't about to stop them.

But if he thought they would flock to hear *Messiah*, as the Dublin audiences had, he was in for a big surprise.

---

[1] Handel in a bad mood was something you wanted to avoid whenever possible. Handel in a good mood could be quite fun, really.

[2] He'd learned his lesson.

The catch was that they tended to be a pretty religious and strait-laced bunch, this rich middle class, and many of them regarded the theatre as a place fit only for good-for-nothings and reprobates. [3] Actors were considered highly suspect (especially ones such as Susannah Cibber, whose exploits were still a chief topic of gossipmongers and tattle-tales).

It wasn't so bad when the oratorios had Old Testament themes. To some degree, people considered those just quaint old stories — history lessons with a strong and uplifting moral at the end. But an oratorio on a *Christian* theme — and in a *theatre*, no less — well, they weren't sure whether that would do at all.

Considering the heights to which *Messiah* has risen and the fervor with which it is now admired, particularly among the religous types in our own day (I ask you, where would the Mormon Tabernacle Choir be today without *Messiah?*) [4], I think it's pretty interesting that Handel's famous oratorio was such a hard sell in those first London years. But it was, so there you go.

The first London performance of *Messiah* was given at the Theatre Royal in Covent Garden on March 23, 1743, with repeat performances on the 25th and 29th. Matthew Dubourg came along from Dublin to lead the orchestra again, and Handel himself conducted.

In hopes of avoiding controversy, the work was not referred to by name in any of the advertisements. It was called simply "A New Sacred Oratorio" or "A Sacred Oratorio."

---

[3] Nowadays we call it Hollywood.
[4] Other than in Salt Lake City, I mean.

Maybe if nobody noticed, Handel thought, they wouldn't get angry.

It was a good plan, but it didn't work. [5]

Even before the performance, there was an uproar in the press. Someone with his nose way out of joint even wrote an angry letter to the *Universal Spectator*:

> "An *Oratorio* is either an *Act of Religion*, or it is not," says the letter, testily; "if it is, I ask if the *Playhouse* is a fit Temple to perform it in, or a Company of Players fit *Ministers* of *God's Word*. ... [I fear] it gives great Opportunity to *profane* Persons to ridicule Religion at least, if not to blaspheme it; [is God's word] to be prostituted to the perverse Humour of a Set of obstinate People?"

And so on.

The letter was signed "Philalethes," which was obviously a pseudonym for somebody or other. Handel scholars aren't sure who. [6]

Well, you could have knocked Handel over with a feather after he'd read that one. And the devout Jennens, too, who would have been mightily surprised to be told that his earnest collection of Bible verses should be considered blasphemous. Really!

---

[5] They never do.

[6] Though I have my suspicions.

Handel didn't bother trying another *Messiah* performance in 1744. There may have been one in 1745, but he definitely gave it a rest again in 1746-48. There was no use flogging a dead horse, the composer always said.

The London audiences finally started coming around for a performance on March 23, 1749. This time it wasn't called "a Sacred Oratorio" or "A New Sacred Oratorio" or anything else. It was *Messiah*, plain and simple, like it or lump it.

But the popularity of *Messiah* didn't really take off until 1750, when Handel began peforming it as a charity fundraiser. Audiences liked to feel that, if they were going to hear something blasphemous, at least they were doing it for a good cause.

From 1750 onwards, Handel mounted an annual production of the work for the Foundling Hospital, a London orphanage. Its full name was the Hospital for the Maintenance and Education of Exposed and Deserted Young Children. Foundling Hospital seems a lot easier.

All told, Handel conducted 11 performances of *Messiah* for the Foundling Hospital, the last one in 1757. From 1758 to '68, the productions were conducted by John Christopher Smith (Jr.), who was Handel's faithful servant and music copyist.[7] From 1769 to '77, the productions were conducted by John Stanley, the famous English blind organist. After that I've lost track.

---

[7] John Christopher Smith Jr. was the son of John Christopher Smith Sr., who had also been Handel's faithful servant and music copyist. Handel had brought them over from Germany, where they'd each started out as Johann Christoph Schmidt.

In the 17 years of Handel's life from his visit to Dublin until his death, there were 56 performances of *Messiah*, including the first two in Dublin, all but 12 of them in theatres or other secular places of entertainment (including one at the Crown and Anchor Tavern, in 1744). In addition to the ones in London, there were performances in Bath, Bristol, Durham, Gloucester, Hereford, Oxford, Salisbury and Worcester. The performance in Hereford Cathedral in 1759 is probably the first time it was ever performed in an actual church. (The 11 Foundling ones were held in the hospital chapel, but that doesn't really count.) [8]

Those 56 performances put *Messiah* well ahead in the race compared to his other oratorios. In Handel's lifetime, *Judas Maccabeus* was performed 34 times, *Samson* 29, *Esther* 22 and *The Occasional Oratorio* only three times. [9]

It may interest you to know, by the way, that *See the conquering hero comes*, the most famous chorus from *Judas Maccabeus*, was originally from one of Handel's earlier oratorios, *Joshua*. Or it may not interest you at all.

For all of the *Messiah* performances Handel conducted, the size of the choir and orchestra was only a little bigger than he'd had in Dublin, and the balance between the forces was pretty much the same. It wasn't till after he died that things started getting out of hand. Account books at the Foundling Hospital show payments made to two French horn

[8] A repeat performance, led by somebody else, in 1744 in Dublin nearly had to be postponed because of the murder trial of Lord Netterville. But Netterville was acquitted, so everything went ahead as planned. I'm sure his Lordship was relieved about that.

[9] That is, only occasionally.

players, but no one's been able to find the parts. Probably they doubled the trumpet parts an octave lower. Or it might have been some sort of scam. [10]

In 1750, the crowd for the Foundling performance was a "very numerous audience." In 1752, it was "a most noble and grand audience." By 1757, it was just a "numerous and polite" audience. They'd heard it already.

Through all of these performances, Handel kept tinkering with the score, most often transposing or rewriting the arias for the benefit of one soloist or another. Sometimes he'd give a soprano one to an alto, or the other way around. Sometimes he'd switch a tenor and soprano around, or whatever seemed to work best at the time.

In 1750, he rewrote *But who may abide the day of his coming?* for the Italian male alto Gaetano Guadagni. It had started out as a simple recitative, but that wasn't enough to show off Guadagni's voice, so Handel transposed it and added a lot more notes, including the whole second section, the flashy bit about the "refiner's fire." Guadagni made it a big hit. ("There is not one shred of evidence," says the famous editor Watkins Shaw, "that he ever gave it to a bass." So there.) [11]

Handel had a bunch of different soloists for his later London performances. Among them were a soprano named Miss Young and a treble called The Boy. (Actually, there

---

[10] "In general, however," Tobin tells us solemnly, "he associated the horns with unbelievers." I'm the same way myself sometimes.

[11] "He was a wild and careless singer," Burney says of Guadagni. But he knew how to wow a crowd. He went on, by the way, to create the title role in Gluck's opera *Orfeo*, which was an important moment in the development of opera, if you care about such things.

were probably several Boys, but Handel never gave them names in the score. One seemed to be the same as any other, as far as he was concerned.) For altos, there were Miss Frederick, Signor Ricciarelli and Mr. Ward. For tenors, he used Beard and Lowe and basses named Reinhold, Savage, Mason and Hill (sounds like a law firm). Lowe's voice was better than Beard's, but he never bothered to learn his notes. Beard had sung as a boy (but not The Boy) in the 1732 production of *Esther*.

In 1759, Beard married Charlotte Rich, the daughter of John Rich, the actor-manager who had produced *The Beggar's Opera*. (There's just no escaping it, is there?)

There were in fact four different Miss Youngs, or Misses Young, and they were all sisters. There was Cecilia, Isabella, Esther and Mary (whose friends called her Polly). Handel never bothered to distinguish one from another in his score, so I'm not about to try. [12]

It was for a *Messiah* performance in 1748 that the soprano Francesca Cuzzoni made a return appearance in England as one of the soloists. She had been a big star in Handel operas in the 1720s — in fact, her celebrated rivalry with another operatic soprano, Faustina Bordoni, had caused riots in the theatres. But by now she was — to put it delicately — considerably past her prime. Let's face it, her voice was shot. It was pretty sad, actually, but everybody applauded politely. What else could they do? [13]

---

[12] Cecilia Young later married Thomas Augustine Arne, which would have made her Susannah Cibber's sister-in-law.

[13] There's been some question over whether Cuzzoni really did or didn't poison her husband, the violinist Sandoni. I'd rather not get into that right now, if you don't mind.

Once she had been a big star, but Cuzzoni ended up moving back to Bologna and working in a button factory. She died flat broke. [14]

It was after hearing the work in London that Thomas Hay, Lord Kinnoull, is said to have congratulated Handel on providing such "a fine entertainment."

"My lord," the composer is said to have replied, "I should be sorry if I only entertained them. I wish to make them better."

There may be no truth whatsoever to this little story, but people like hearing it anyway. It sounds so clever.

Speaking of questionable anecdotes, it was of course for one of those London performances of *Messiah* that King George (that would have been George II by then) is said to have begun the tradition of standing for the duration of the *Hallelujah* chorus, (sometimes referred to as "The Hooray Chorus.") [15]

Standing for the *Hallelujah* chorus is a tradition that continues to this day, whether we want it to or not.

The whole thing's rather silly, if you ask me, and I don't care who knows it. No one's quite sure how it got started. The "official" version is that George was so moved by the glory of the music that he stood in reverence, and that we should all do the same. It's just as likely, knowing George, that his foot had gone to sleep and he stood up to get the

---

[14] I'd been hoping to work up to a joke here about buttons and Samson and "eyelets in Gaza" — but it seems like an awful lot of trouble for one bad pun, so maybe I won't bother.

[15] Interestingly enough, in Handel's day the famous chorus was known as *For the Lord God omnipotent reigneth*. It wasn't until later that it began to be called the *Hallelujah* chorus. Probably some printer trying to save space.

circulation going, or that he arrived late (George was always arriving late for things), and everybody stood up because that's what you have to do whenever the king enters the room. But you know how it is: once the king stands up, everybody has to stand up. [16]

This whole standing business wouldn't bother me nearly so much if people actually knew why they were doing it. I mean, if they too felt genuinely moved by the grandeur and solemnity of it all and felt they just had to stand out of respect, that wouldn't be so bad. But the trouble is, most people do it just because they think somehow they're supposed to. Or they see other people around them standing up, and they do it too so they won't feel stupid being the only ones sitting down. It's like one of those half-hearted standing ovations that starts at the front of the hall and progresses, grudgingly, in dribs and drabs through the rest of the audience, not because of genuine appreciation, but out of an awkward sense of social obligation. Anyway, it's a dumb tradition and I won't stand for it.

Handel was a large man all around, tall and portly and rather bear-like and slightly bow-legged. He scowled a lot of the time but he had a nice smile if you caught him in the right mood, and sometimes he'd laugh so hard his wig would nearly fall off. He had a quick temper and was not above shouting and stamping his foot impatiently if things weren't going his way. He absolutely hated listening to instruments tuning up, and once got so fed up with it that he threw a kettledrum

[16] Or maybe George had just clued in to the words of the earlier solo *Why do the nations?* in which the bass sings: "The kings of the earth rise up."

clear across the room, which made his wig fall off completely. [17]

But he was a nice guy, really, once you got past the gruff exterior. We all have our bad days, I guess.

Handel never married, though the biographer W.S. Rockstro tells us quite confidently that he was engaged at least three times. Where Rockstro gets this I'm not sure, since other biographers don't mention it, but just for the record here's the scoop: Handel was engaged the first time to a woman named Vittoria Tesi, back when he was a young man travelling in Italy. Later, he was engaged to a young English woman, but the mother didn't want her daughter marrying a musician, so that was the end of that. And he was also supposedly engaged to another English woman "of large property," but she wanted him to give up music entirely, so he walked away from that one.

Thanks largely to the popularity of *Messiah*, Handel's last years were spent in relative comfort. He didn't have to worry so much anymore about money and his fame was once again secure. He grew extremely stout and began more and more to resemble that infamous Goupy caricature.

He did tend to mutter quite a lot to himself and his eyesight got worse and worse until he went completely blind, but all in all he was generally happy. [18]

---

[17] Handel's tuning fork was pitched at A 422.5, a little bit lower than the present A 440. This may have had something to do with it.

[18] Handel's eyesight got even worse after he was operated on by John Taylor, an English quack. Taylor had done similar favors for both J.S. Bach and the historian Edward Gibbon.

Handel died on April 14, 1759, in between the *Messiah* performances at Covent Garden on April 6 and the Foundling Hospital on May 3. The Covent Garden performance April 6 was the last time he heard *Messiah* performed. He left a copy of the score to the Foundling Hospital so the charity concerts could continue.

There are more than 16 versions of *Messiah* from Handel's day in manuscript form, either in his own handwriting or his copyist's or someone else's. There's the Autograph Score, the Tenbury Copy, the Foundling Copy, the Barrett-Lennard Copy, the Barclay Squire Aylesford Copy and on and on. Not one of them agrees entirely with the others. It's this kind of thing that keeps Handel scholars in business. [19]

Handel is buried in Westminster Abbey, where there's a lovely monument by Louis Francois Roubiliac erected to him, showing the great composer busily at work writing *I know that my Redeemer liveth*. [20]

The composer who had twice declared bankruptcy earlier in his career died with nearly £20,000 in the bank and a nice Brook Street house filled with furniture and manuscripts and scraps of staff paper all over the place. He also owned a lovely Ruckers harpsichord with a picture on the sound board of some little monkeys giving a concert, and two Rembrandt

---

[19] So I guess I shouldn't complain, either.

[20] Handel paid for it himself, leaving money for it in his will "not Exceeding Six Hundred Pounds." He had his pride, but he was also practical. He may have wanted a lasting monument, but he figured there was no sense squandering a fortune on one if he wasn't going to be around to appreciate it.

paintings, which he bequeathed to Bernard Granville. [21]

The household inventory taken at the time of his death says that Handel owned, among other things, several beds with pillows and bolsters, some chairs for the dining room, a big desk, an easy chair, a bunch of brass candelsticks, six china saucers but only five cups, and an old blue and white china spoon boat. His servant John Duburk bought the whole shebang for £48 — including the house, apparently, which made it quite a bargain.

I wonder whatever happened to that sixth china cup?

[21] This was less generous than it sounds. Granville had given one of them to Handel in the first place.

CHAPTER 8

MILESTONE
OR MILLSTONE?

Singalong Messiah

MILESTONE
OR MILLSTONE?

A FTER HANDEL'S DEATH the popularity of *Messiah* just grew and grew. In the years immediately following, there were performances in Cambridge, Birmingham, Bury St. Edmunds and all over the place.

Once the first full score was published in 1767 and performers stopped having to rely on one of the hand-copied manuscripts, the number of performances really took off. It got so nearly anyone could perform *Messiah*, or at least try to. And nearly anyone did. Or tried.

And as the oratorio's popularity grew, so did the number of musicians involved in performing it. For the Foundling Hospital performance in 1771, for example, the usual choir of 30 or so trained singers was joined by "26 Chorus Singers Volunteers not paid." This is what professional singers refer to as a Dangerous Trend. For the first time, the singers began to significantly outnumber the players in the orchestra, paving the way for the massive choirs that were to come later. This is what orchestral players refer to as a Dangerous Trend.

Things started getting really out of hand in 1784, at two special commemorative performances in Westminster Abbey, to mark the 25th anniversary of Handel's burial there and, incidentally, the upcoming centennary of his birth in 1685. There were about 500 performers, more than half of them singers, the rest in the orchestra.

Interestingly, the choruses were still almost entirely made up of males, with only a few sopranos helping out the boy trebles. Other than as soloists, women had not yet made any inroads into the alto section. (It wasn't long, however, before women began to outnumber men in the alto sections. By the 19th century, the balance had almost entirely shifted. Nowadays, it's rare to find male altos in the chorus, and they hardly ever show up as soloists, except in "authentic" performances.)

The Westminster Abbey gigs were held to raise money for Handel's pet charity, the one for "Decay'd Musicians," of which he had been a charter member (and was by now a prime example).

The first performance of *Messiah* outside the British Empire took place in Germany, in Hamburg in 1772. That performance, in English, was conducted by Michael Arne, the illegitimate son of Thomas Augustine Arne. That would make him the illegitimate stepson of the soprano soloist Cecilia Arne, the former Miss Young (one of them, anyway), and some sort of nephew to Susannah Cibber. J.S. Bach's boy C.P.E. Bach conducted the first performance of the work translated into German, in 1775. [1]

---

[1] When he wasn't conducting or composing, Michael Arne spent a great deal of his time searching for the legendary Philosopher's Stone, which would magically turn base metals into gold. He never found it, obviously.

The first full performance of *Messiah* in North America seems to have been in Boston, on Christmas Day, in 1818, although the *Hallelujah* chorus and other excerpts had been performed in New York as early as 1770. The first account I've found of any complete performance in Canada was in February 1873 by the Toronto Philharmonic Society.

Handel hadn't been dead even for 30 years before other composers started getting it into their heads to add more instruments to the orchestra. The best-known of these "orchestral" versions is the one Mozart produced in 1789, which was published in Leipzig in 1803 a few years after his death. An orchestrator named Robert Franz "completed" the Mozart score by adding trombone parts, and a few other things, in 1885. Franz thought there was nothing like a few trombones to really liven things up a little.

Expanding the orchestra may make the sound bigger and more impressive, but it may not be exactly what Handel had in mind. (Although others will argue, quite convincingly, that if Handel had had access to clarinets and trombones and double bassoons and so on at the time, he'd have used them, too. Who knows? Maybe he would have. After all, he used live sparrows as a special effect in the production of his opera *Rinaldo*, back in 1711.)

But whichever side of the argument you may believe, the purists among you shouldn't blame Mozart for all of the instrumental additions.

"It is fairly safe to assume," musicologist John Tobin tells us earnestly, "that Johann Adam Hiller, sometimes known as 'The Father of the Singspiel,' must take the blame for the less worthy additions."

Among those "less worthy" moments is the one in *If God be for us* that changes Handel's violin obbligato solo into "a vulgar bassoon obbligato." (Whether by that Tobin means a vulgar obbligato for bassoon, or an obbligato for vulgar bassoon, is not clear. At any rate, he doesn't like it and neither do I.) [2]

Interestingly, Mozart also had to rewrite the accompaniment for *The trumpet shall sound*, not only because Handel's high-registered Baroque trumpet solo was considered too tricky, but also because in German, in the Lutheran Bible, it isn't a trumpet you're going to hear at the Last Judgment, but a *posaune*, or trombone. Somehow, the sound of a heavenly trombone doesn't conjure up the right image for me, but who am I to argue? [3]

One of the fascinating changes in *Messiah* traditions since Handel's death is the time of year with which it is most often associated. Nowadays, that's almost invariably at Christmastime, and the annual dose of *Messiah* has become as much a Christmas tradition as mistletoe, plum pudding, stockings by the fire, *A Christmas Carol*, *It's a Wonderful Life*, Santa Claus, *Rudolph the red-nosed reindeer* and all the rest of the jumbled collection of Christmas lore.

Yet Handel himself associated it not with Christmas but with Lent, or Easter. The performances in Handel's own lifetime took place around Easter or during Lent, the period leading up to it. (It's no coincidence that in London at that time the opera houses were usually closed during Lent, since

[2] Obbligato, of course, is the fancy Italian term for an instrument one is obligated, or obliged, to use. If you don't, there's always the risk the composer might come around and break your kneecaps or something.

[3] Robert Franz would probably have loved it.

opera was deemed insufficiently penitential. And notwithstanding any controversy over *Messiah,* it was certainly considered at least a little more appropriate for that time of the Christian calendar. Handel was no fool, and he knew a marketing opportunity when it was staring him in the face.)

It's unlikely, however, despite the drive toward historical authenticity, that we'll see a big push to move the oratorio away from Christmas productions, so don't hold your breath.

By a century after Handel's death, *Messiah* performances had begun to get really huge. The Handel Festival performances held at the Crystal Palace in London in 1857, and annually beginning in 1859, had choirs approaching 5,000 singers, with full-blown orchestras as backup. There were sometimes 10,000 people in the audience. I hope there were enough washrooms.

The trend to "orchestral" performances was popularized even more by the publication in 1902 of the full-score edition by Ebenezer Prout, with all the bells and whistles. There are still copies floating around in use today, though fewer and fewer people take them seriously. [4]

But even in the 19th century there were a few courageous people complaining that *Messiah* was becoming too bloated and reverential for its own good.

"I have long since recognized the impossibility of obtaining justice for that work in a Christian country," playwright and music critic George Bernard Shaw wrote in a newspaper review in 1891. (Shaw, by the way, was a great

---

[4] Prout, along with Scrooge, must be one of the few well-known people ever to be named Ebenezer.

admirer of Handel, and considered *Messiah* his favorite oratorio.) The problem, as Shaw saw it, was that everyone sang the work far too much in earnest, in the "churchgoing mood" of "pure abstract reverence."

What the work really needs, says Shaw, is a little wild abandon. "Import a choir of heathens," he writes, "restrained by no considerations of propriety from attacking the choruses with unembarrassed sincerity of dramatic expression, and I would hasten to the performance if only to witness the delight of the public and discomfiture of the critics."

Even as early as 1891, Shaw had the foresight to call for a historically accurate performance of Handel's great work.

"Why, instead of wasting huge sums on the multitudinous dullness called a Handel Festival," writes Shaw, "does not somebody set up a thoroughly rehearsed and exhaustively studied performance of *The Messiah* in St. James's Hall with a chorus of twenty capable artists? Most of us would be glad to hear the work seriously performed once before we die." [5]

Alas, although he lived a long time, dying in 1950 at the age of 94, Shaw never really got his wish to hear a "chamber" performance of the work. (There was a pioneering version in 1894 in Cambridge, but evidently Shaw didn't know about it.)

The forces of legitimacy got a tremendous boost in 1959 with the publication by Novello of the scholarly yet accessible version of the score edited by Watkins Shaw. It's the standard version now in use almost everywhere.

---

[5] Those of you looking for ammunition in the fight over *Messiah* and *The Messiah* should feel free to recruit Bernard Shaw to your cause, by the way. He has impressive credentials.

But even so, the tendency towards large-scale productions continues, kept alive by amateur choral societies, as well as by the Mormon Tabernacle Choir and other big groups. It's just so much fun, and everybody wants to get into the act.

One of ways of letting more people join in the fun is the "singalong" *Messiah*, which has become increasingly popular. People bring their own scores, sit in the audience and sing along with a choir in the choruses, sometimes interspersed with soloists performing the arias. A sort of karaoke *Messiah*, if you like. This kind of thing makes purists cringe (having done a few, I'll admit it makes me a bit uncomfortable), but there's no denying its popular appeal.

What we have now in *Messiah* circles, in fact, is a two-tiered system of performances. On the one hand are the smaller, more historically accurate "authentic" productions, often using period instruments or accurate reproductions, and sometimes male altos as soloists and in the chorus (and sometimes boy sopranos, too). On the other hand are the bigger, splashier productions with a large chorus, a full orchestra and full ranks of women in the soprano and alto sections and as soloists. This is definitely still the more popular of the two, though the "period" version is winning increasing converts.

I suppose there's room for both (he said magnanimously), though I can't help wondering what Handel himself must be thinking about the whole dilemma. Maybe someone should try asking him. His last known address was Westminster Abbey, over in the south transept, right underneath the big statue. You can't miss it.

CHAPTER 9

CODA

There are those who think Messiah
has been done to death

CODA

I T'S BEEN MORE THAN 250 years since Handel
composed *Messiah*, and in that time it's had thousands — probably many tens of thousands — of performances all over the world.

Add to that the hundreds of different recordings, the
radio and television broadcasts too numerous to be counted,
the people humming *Hallelujah* and *All we like sheep* as
they walk down the street, the "greatest-hits" selections piped
over the Muzak systems of elevators and shopping malls
everywhere, and you begin to understand the magnitude of
its appeal and influence. It's to the point now where you
probably couldn't get away from it even if you tried.

And believe me, I've tried.

Like many musicians, I've developed a typical love/hate
relationship with *Messiah* over the years, from having performed it more times than I can remember (both as a soloist
and in the chorus) and from having heard it, or snatches of
it, even more often than that.

At its best, when performed really well, I know that

Handel's great oratorio can be impressive, majestic, playful and incredibly moving — both musically and spiritually — all at once. But at its worst, performed badly, it can come across as hokey, repetitive, lead-footed and incredibly dull.

This isn't the fault of the music so much as of the musicians, I know, but if you're sitting through yet another long boring stretch, it's hard to remember not to blame the music for sounding that way.

The problem is that *Messiah* has been done to death. Too many musicians — singers and instrumentalists — have performed it so many times that it's hard not to just go through the motions of playing (or singing) the notes, rather than remembering that you have to turn the notes into real music.

The other problem with *Messiah* is an inherent paradox. Musically, not to mention emotionally, it is at one and the same time both an *easy* and a difficult piece of music to perform. On the purely technical side, there are a lot of notes, and many of them whiz by pretty quickly, making them difficult to sing. And there are other sections for both the chorus and orchestra that require extreme accuracy in tuning, blend and ensemble. And many of the solos require singers of exceptional skill.

It may not be as demanding on its performers as Bach's *B-minor Mass*, (in my book the most difficult masterpiece in the entire choral repertoire), but *Messiah* is no slouch. It's a difficult work to pull off.

On the other hand, everybody knows it — or they think they know it, anyway — and they like it so much, and it's become such a tradition, that they're happy to take a stab at it, because they think it will be easy and fun.

Too often, the result is a vast undertaking done in a half-vast way, where most of the performers manage to fool most of the people (and themselves) most of the time.

Some performances, unfortunately, seem to echo the lines from that Yeats poem, in which "the best lack all conviction, while the worst are full of passionate intensity."

In addition, of course, *Messiah* has reached such heights of reverence, both from musicians and listeners, that it has become the Sacred Cow of the musical repertoire. Say anything bad about *Messiah*, or even complain when it is performed less than perfectly, and you risk being branded a spoilsport, or a cretin or (horrors!) a blasphemer. (Interesting how things have changed: 250 years ago, Philalethes was accusing anyone who supported *Messiah* of blasphemy. Now the opposite is true.)

Anyway, one thing is for sure. We're not about to hear the last of *Messiah* for quite a long time yet. I'm sure Handel would be pleased to know that his little oratorio has reached such heights of popularity, and is performed so widely and so often by every Tom, Dick and Ebenezer.

Still, I'm not at all sure this is what he had in mind when he wrote it. But maybe it was.

Maybe he knew that, if he played his cards right, he could write something that would win over its audiences and make him a little money. *Messiah* did that in spades.

And it will probably keep on doing it — until the last trump.

The Author

David Barber is a journalist and musician and the author of four previous books of musical humor. Formerly entertainment editor of *The Kingston Whig-Standard*, Barber is now a freelance writer, composer and performer, and the proprietor of White Knight Books, a secondhand bookstore in Westport, Ontario. His compositions include two symphonies, a jazz mass based on the music of Dave Brubeck, various chamber and choral works and numerous vocal-jazz arrangements. He also enjoys kayaking, canoeing and blending tea.

The Illustrator

Dave Donald can't remember when he didn't scrawl his little marks on most surfaces, so it doesn't come as much of a surprise that he now makes a living doing just that. He is currently balancing a steady job as art director for a Toronto magazine publisher with his other more abstruse artistic pursuits. This book represents Dave's fifth illustrative collaboration with David Barber.

Other books by David W. Barber,
illustrated by Dave Donald

A MUSICIAN'S DICTIONARY (1983)
ISBN 0-920151-03-5

BACH, BEETHOVEN, AND THE BOYS (1986)
Music History As It Ought To Be Taught
ISBN 0-920151-07-8

WHEN THE FAT LADY SINGS (1990)
Opera History As It Ought To Be Taught
ISBN 0-920151-11-6

IF IT AIN'T BAROQUE (1992)
More Music History As It Ought To Be Taught
ISBN 0-920151-15-9

by Dave Donald

HECTOR AND THE BIG HOUSE (1977)

Getting A Handel On Messiah

First published in Canada by

SOUND AND VISION PUBLISHING LIMITED
359 Riverdale Avenue
Toronto, Canada M4J 1A4

First printing for Xmas of 1994
14 12 10 8 6 4 2 - printings - 1 3 5 7 9 11 13 15
98 96 94 - history - 95 97 99

Canadian Cataloguing in Publication Data

Barber, David W. (David William), 1958 -
Getting a Handel on Messiah
ISBN 0-920151-17-5
1. Handel, George Frideric, 1685-1759. Messiah.
2. Handel, George Frideric, 1685-1759 - Humor
1. Donald, David C. 11. Title.

ML410.HI3B37 1994   782.23'092   C94-932031-5

Typeset in ITC Souvenir
Printed and bound in Canada on acid-free paper

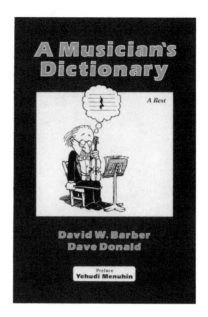

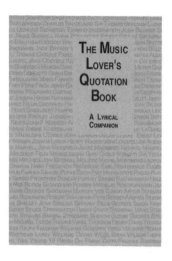

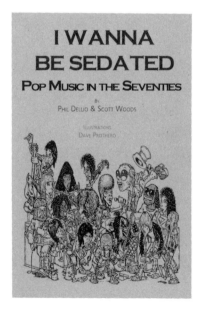

I WANNA
BE SEDATED
POP MUSIC IN THE SEVENTIES

BY
PHIL DELLIO & SCOTT WOODS

ILLUSTRATIONS
DAVE PROTHERO

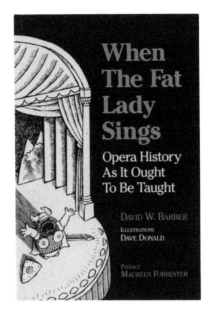

When The Fat Lady Sings

Opera History
As It Ought
To Be Taught

DAVID W. BARBER

ILLUSTRATIONS
DAVE DONALD

PREFACE
MAUREEN FORRESTER

IF IT AIN'T BAROQUE...

MORE Music History As It
Ought To Be Taught

DAVID W. BARBER

ILLUSTRATIONS
DAVE DONALD

If you have any comments
on this book or any other books
that we publish, please write to us at
Sound And Vision 359 Riverdale Avenue
Toronto, Canada M4J 1A4